MW00395665

Printed By Createspace, An Amazon.com Company

Made in the
USA
Columbia, SC

81658536R00074